NnOoPp
QqRr
SsTtUu
VvWw
XxYyZz

volume **8**

BIG BIRD'S SESAME STREET DICTIONARY

FEATURING JIM HENSON'S SESAME STREET MUPPETS

LETTERS T–Z

by Linda Hayward

illustrated by Joe Mathieu

Editor in Chief: Sharon Lerner

Art Directors: Grace Clarke and Cathy Goldsmith
with special thanks to Judith M. Leary

Funk & Wagnalls, Inc./Children's Television Workshop

T t

A B C D E F G H I J K L M N O P Q R S **T** U V W X Y Z

table   A table is a piece of furniture with a flat top and legs.

Lay your cards on the **table,** Rosie!

tail   A tail is a part of an animal's body. Some animals have tails and some animals do not.

Different animals have different kinds of **tails.**

I'm an animal, but I don't have a **tail.**

take   When you take something, you catch hold of it, or have it with you when you go somewhere. Take also means do or make.

Oh, Mommy, I am so scared of the dark.

Don't be frightened, Grover, dear. **Take** my hand and I will **take** you home. Then you can **take** your bath.

talk   When you talk, you say words.

Biff likes to **talk.** Sully likes to listen.

Hey, Sully, what do you have in your lunchbox? I have a peanut butter sandwich. I love peanut butter....

tall Something tall is long from top to bottom. It is not short. The height of something is how tall it is.

I'm tall.

I'm taller.

I'm tallest.

taste When you taste something, you find out what flavor it has. You taste things with your tongue.

I can **taste** this lemon. It is sour.

I can **taste** this lollipop. It is sweet.

taxi A taxi is a special kind of car. You pay a taxi driver to drive you somewhere.

Bert and Ernie are going on a trip. They are taking a **taxi** to the airport.

teach When you teach, you help someone to learn.

teacher A teacher is someone who teaches—usually at a school.

Grover's **teacher** is trying to **teach** him how to write his name.

team A team is a group of people who work together to do the same thing.

My **team** is winning!

tear   A tear is a tiny drop of water that comes from your eye when you cry.

Farley has **tears** in his eyes. He is crying because he dropped his apple in the sandbox.

tear   When you tear something, you pull it apart.

I like to **tear** paper because **torn** paper is one of my favorite kinds of trash.

rrrrip!

telephone   A telephone is used to send or receive sounds. When you use a telephone, you can talk to someone who is far away.

Big Bird is talking to Granny Bird on the **telephone.**

Gee, Granny. I sure like the birdseed cookies you sent to me.

I sure like the picture you sent to *me*, Big Bird.

television   A television is a machine. When you turn on a television, you can see people and things and hear the sounds they make.

Bert is watching his favorite show on **television.**

tell   When you tell something, you put it into words.

temperature   The temperature of something is how hot or how cold it is. You use a thermometer to measure temperature.

Grover has a thermometer in his mouth. His mother is taking his **temperature.**

Don't feel bad, Grover, dear. I will **tell** you a story.

Goldilocks and the Three Bears

ten   Ten is a number. Ten is one more than nine.

I have **ten** bats in my belfry.

10

thank When you thank someone, you say you like what that person did for you.

Gee, Barkley, I want to **thank** you for finding my other shoe.

that That means which or the one there.

LET'S MAKE A CHOICE!

Hi, folks! It's time to play— LET'S MAKE A CHOICE! Today's contestant is Betty Lou. Betty Lou, what's your choice— this or **that**?

I choose **that**.

THAT

THIS

Let's see what's inside the package **that** Betty Lou chose. It's ...

a year's supply of trash from Oscar the Grouch! Better luck next time, Betty Lou!

THAT

THIS

If you want to see Betty Lou play this game again, look up the words these, this, and those.

the The means a certain one.

Bert, have you seen Rubber Duckie?

Do you mean **the** rubber duckie that I found in my paper clip collection, Ernie?

theater A theater is a place where you can see a play or a movie or another kind of show.

The Count is arriving at the **theater**.

NOW PLAYING... A THOUSAND AND ONE ARABIAN NIGHTS

TICKETS

their Their is another way of saying belonging to them. When something is theirs, it belongs to them.

them Them is another way of saying the ones I am talking about.

The Busbys are sitting on **their** bicycle.

This bicycle is mine. That bicycle is **theirs**. It belongs to **them**.

then   Then means at that time.

there   There means in that place.

these   These means the ones here.

they   They means the people or things I am talking about.

thick When something solid is thick, it is big from side to side. When something liquid is thick, it is gooey and hard to pour.

thin When something is thin, it is not thick.

thing A thing can be seen or heard or touched or smelled. A thing can also be done or said or thought of.

Hand me that **thick** board, Sully. This board is too **thin**.

This paint is too **thick**.

This paint is too **thin**.

By the way, what is this **thing** we're building?

think When you think, you use your mind.

Hey, Bert. Does this beach umbrella make you **think** of building sand castles?

No, Ernie. It makes me **think** of vacuuming the rug. That beach umbrella was full of sand before you opened it.

thirsty When you are thirsty, you want something to drink.

Marshal Grover and Fred are **thirsty.**

Here you are— two big glasses of milk!

thirteen Thirteen is a number. Thirteen is ten plus three more.

Bert has three big boxes of oatmeal and ten small boxes of oatmeal. He has **thirteen** boxes of oatmeal all together.

this   This means the one here.

those   Those means the ones there.

LET'S MAKE A CHOICE!

Here's our contestant, Betty Lou, back to play— LET'S MAKE A CHOICE! Once more, Betty Lou . . . what do you choose **this** or that or these or **those**?

This or that? These or **those**? **Those** or these? **This** or that? AARRRGGGHH! I can't stand it. Nothing! I choose nothing!

Then let's see what you did not choose. In **this** package we find— a little puppy! In that package we find—a large bag of jellybeans! In these packages we find— cute, adorable kittens! And in **those** packages—a year's supply of coconut cream pies! I'm sorry, Betty Lou. And thanks for being such a wonderful contestant.

If you want to see what Betty Lou is thinking, look up the word thought.

thought   A thought is an idea. A thought is what someone thinks.

Betty Lou's **thought:**

thread   A thread is a thin piece of string used for sewing.

three   Three is a number. Three is one more than two.

Farley is sewing **three** buttons on his shirt with **thread.**

through Through means from one side to the other side or from one end to the other end of something.

Barkley can jump **through** a hoop.

Through also means finished.

Are you **through** with that dictionary? I need it.

throw When you throw something, you toss it through the air.

When I **throw** the stick, Barkley runs after it.

thumb Your thumb is one of the fingers on your hand. Look up the word hand.

Ernie, why do you have a string tied around your **thumb**?

So I won't forget to buy more string.

thunder Thunder is the loud noise you sometimes hear when there is lightning. Look up the word lightning.

KA-BOOM!

Ahh. One lovely bolt of lightning and one fabulous clap of **thunder**! Wonderful!

ticket A ticket is a piece of paper that allows you to do something. Sometimes you pay money for a ticket.

tickle When something tickles you, it touches you lightly and makes you laugh.

Big Bird is riding on the train. The conductor is taking his **ticket.**

Feathers can **tickle.**

Hee hee hee ho ho ho ha ha ha ha hoo hoo hoo

tie When you tie a string, rope, or ribbon, you put a knot or bow in it.

Ernie can **tie** his shoelaces.

A **tie** is something you can wear around your neck.

tiger A tiger is a big, wild orange cat with black stripes.

> I've always wondered if a **tiger** is orange with black stripes, or black with orange stripes.

> I don't think I'll wait to find out.

ROAR!

tight When something is tight, it fits too closely. It is not loose.

> My Uncle Charlie knitted this nice sweater for me. But he must not know how much I've grown. Look how **tight** it is.

time Time is when something happens. Time is measured in seconds, minutes, hours, days, weeks, months, and years.

> What **time** is it, Ernie?

> It's six o'clock, Bert.

> Oh, good! It's **time** for the Pigeon News.

> If you have a good **time**, you enjoy yourself. If you have a good **time**, you enjoy yourself.

> He said that two **times**.

tired When you are tired, you need to rest.

> YAWN! Oh, dear. I am **tired**. I think I will go home to take my nap.

to To means in the direction of.

Betty Lou is throwing a ball **to** Barkley.

today Today is the day it is now.

> **Today** is my birthday. **Today** everyone does everything just the way I like it. No cake, no presents, and nobody saying HAPPY BIRTHDAY.

toe Your toe is a part of your foot. You have five toes on each foot. Look up the word body.

Bert is doing his exercises. He is touching his **toes**.

together Together means with each other.

tomato A tomato is a round red fruit that grows on vines above the ground.

Tomato

> Hi, Oscar! We are all here **together** because it's your birthday today.

> And here's a present from all of us.

> Wow! It's a rotten **tomato.** It's just what I wanted. Gee, thanks, everyone, for such a perfect birthday.

> Here is a cake made out of mud.

Have a Rotten Birthday

tomorrow Tomorrow is the day that comes after today.

> I can't wait until **tomorrow.** Granny Bird just said she is coming to visit.

click

tongue Your tongue is a part of your mouth. It helps you speak and taste.

> Barkley likes to taste ice cream with his **tongue.**

tonight Tonight is the night of the day that it is now.

> **Tonight** I can see stars in the sky. That is the Big Dipper.

too Too means also.

> What is blue and furry and lovable and has eight wheels?

> Grover on roller skates!

> And I am *cute,* **too.**

too   Too can also mean more than enough.

tool   A tool is used to do work. Here are some different kinds of tools.

pencil

hammer

can opener

knife

hand drill

pliers

scissors

paper clip

wrench

screwdriver

saw

spade

ax

hedge clippers

sewing needle

Tools Help People Work

Can you match the tools with the workers who use them?

tooth   A tooth is one of your teeth. Teeth are in your mouth and are used for biting and chewing.

Frazzle is brushing his **teeth**. He has one **tooth**brush for each **tooth**.

top   The top of something is its highest part.

Where did you put my ball, Bert?

It's on the **top** of the toy chest, Ernie.

A **top** is also a lid. My jar has a blue **top**.

touch   When you touch something, you feel it with your hand or another part of your body.

I love to **touch** my little lamb. He feels so soft.

towel   A towel is a piece of cloth or paper that is used for drying something wet.

Herry Monster took a shower. He is drying himself with a **towel**.

town   A town is a place where many people live and work. A town is usually smaller than a city.

Marshal Grover is riding into **town**.

toy   A toy is something to play with.

Three of these things belong together. One of these things is not the same.

Rubber Duckie, a toy airplane, and a jack-in-the box are all **toys**. Bert's shoe is something to wear. Bert's shoe does not belong.

train   A train is a string of railroad cars pulled along a track by an engine.

The cars have to stop so the **train** can go by.

trash   Trash is things that are thrown away.

travel   When you travel, you go from one place to another.

> Whenever I **travel**, I collect **trash** on the way.

ROAD CLOSED

tree   A tree is a tall plant with a woody stem called a trunk. A tree has branches and leaves or needles.

Who is hiding behind each **tree**?

palm tree

maple tree

pine tree

triangle   A triangle is a shape with three sides and three corners.

Three of these things belong together.
One of these things is not the same.
The square has four sides and four corners.
The square does not belong.

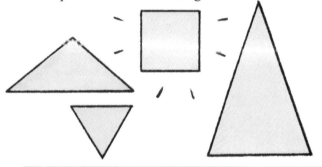

trick   A trick is a clever thing you can do.

The Amazing Mumford is doing a magic **trick.**

tricycle   A tricycle is something to ride. It has three wheels, a seat, handlebars, and pedals.

Barkley can ride a **tricycle.**

That is a good trick for a dog!

trip   When you go on a trip, you travel somewhere.

Farley is going on a **trip.** He is taking the train.

Have a nice **trip,** Farley.

trip   When you trip, your foot bumps into something and you stumble or fall.

Grover, dear, be careful not to **trip** on the roller skate.

Oooops! You **tripped.**

trouble   When you are having trouble, you are having a problem.

Hey, Bert! I'm having **trouble** moving this box. What's in it?

Ernie, that's where I keep my rock collection.

truck A truck is a machine with an engine and four or more wheels. It is used to carry loads or do other kinds of work.

> I just love to count **trucks.**

true When something is true, it is real. It is not false or a lie.

> Is it **true** that a whale is the largest animal?

> It's **true.**

trunk A trunk is a big suitcase.

trunk A trunk is also an elephant's nose.

trunk A trunk can also be the woody stem of a tree.

> I, the Amazing Mumford, will now pull from this perfectly empty **trunk** two other **trunks.**

> A LA PEANUT BUTTER SANDWICHES!

> 1, 2, 3... three **trunks**! Amazing!

try When you try to do something, you make an effort to do it.

> I, Grover Knover, will **try** to jump over this pond.

> Nice **try,** Grover Knover!

> **Try** again.

turn When something turns, it goes around and around or changes direction.

When I ride my bicycle, the wheels **turn** very fast.

When I **turn** a corner, I change direction.

turn When one thing turns into another thing, it becomes something else.

When water freezes, it **turns** into ice.

ice cubes

water

turtle A turtle is an animal with a hard shell and a soft body. A turtle can pull its head and arms and legs inside its shell.

Some people say that **turtles** can hide inside their shells and look just like rocks. Do you believe that?

Oh!

twelve Twelve is a number. Twelve is ten plus two more.

Bert has ten blue shoelaces and two orange shoelaces. Bert has **twelve** shoelaces all together.

Twelve things make a dozen.

twenty Twenty is a number. Twenty is ten plus ten more.

Ernie has ten red jellybeans and ten green jellybeans. Ernie has **twenty** jellybeans all together.

twin A twin is one of two children who have the same mother and father and are born at the same time. Some twins look exactly alike. Some twins do not look like each other.

The Busby **twins** look alike.

The Henderson **twins** do not look alike.

two Two is a number. Two is one more than one.

There are **two** Busby twins.

This dictionary is not as terrible as I thought. The T section has rotten tomatoes, garbage trucks, and trash, trash, trash!

Uu

A B C D E F G H I J K L M N O P Q R S T **U** V W X Y Z

ugly   When you think something is ugly, you do not like to look at it or hear it.

Oscar, please clean up this **ugly** pile of trash.

Ugly? I think it's beautiful.

umbrella   An umbrella is a folding cover that protects you from the rain or the sun.

When can three big monsters fit under a tiny **umbrella** and not get wet?

When it is not raining.

RRRR!

uncle   Your uncle is the brother of your mother or your father. Your aunt's husband is also your uncle.

Uncle Bob

Uncle Lew

Uncle Bob is my mother's brother. **Uncle** Lew is my father's brother.

Mother

Father

Me

under   Under means below.

Super Grover is flying **under** the bridge. Little Bird is flying over the bridge.

understand When you understand something, you know what it means.

I don't **understand** what that word means.

Now I **understand.** Agua means water.

underwear The clothes you wear under your other clothes are called underwear. Undershirts and underpants are two kinds of underwear.

There are stars on the Amazing Mumford's **underwear.**

undress When you undress, you take off your clothes.

Ernie must **undress** before he can take a bath.

unhappy When you are unhappy, you do not feel happy—you feel sad.

Bert is **unhappy.** He lost his whole bottle cap collection.

until Until means up to the time of.

Farmer Grover always waits at the gate **until** the cows come home.

unusual Unusual means not usual. Something that is unusual is something that you are not used to seeing or hearing or feeling.

No, thank you.

Cookie Monster doesn't want any cookies. That is **unusual.**

up When you go up, you move to a higher place.

I am going **up** the ladder.

I am going down the ladder.

upside down When something is upside down, the top is on the bottom and the bottom is on the top.

Big Bird is **upside down.**

us Us is another way of saying you and me.

Look, Ernie! Here is a package for **us.**

Bert & Ernie 123 Sesame St.

use When you use a thing, you do something with it.

Hey, Bert. What does the word **use** mean?

Let's **use** the dictionary to find out.

usual Something that is usual is something that you are used to seeing, hearing, or feeling.

Bert is having his **usual** breakfast.

Bert, are you having oatmeal for breakfast *again*?

—YUM!

usually Usually means most often or in the ordinary way.

I **usually** complain at the end of each letter. So here I go. Where are all those other U words— like unbearable, unclean, unfriendly, unsightly, untidy, and unwelcome? This dictionary is unfair to us grouches!

Vv

A B C D E F G H I J K L M N O P Q R S T U **V** W X Y Z

vacation   A vacation is a special time when someone does not work or go to school.

Guy Smiley is on **vacation.**

vacuum   When you vacuum, you use a vacuum cleaner to suck up dust and dirt.

HUMMM

Bert likes to **vacuum** the rug.

valentine   A valentine is a card that you send on Valentine's Day to someone you like.

To My Friend Snuffy

Big Bird sent Snuffle-upagus a **valentine** on the fourteenth of February.

vase   A vase is a container used for holding flowers.

Mr. Snuffle-upagus sent me a flower for Valentine's Day.

Big Bird put his flower in a **vase.**

vegetable   A vegetable is a plant that is used for food.

Farmer Grover is picking **vegetables** in his **vegetable** garden.

vehicle   A vehicle is something that can carry people or things from one place to another. Wagons, automobiles, trucks, and sleds are different kinds of vehicles.

I love to count **vehicles.**

very Very means more than usual or much.

My dog is big, but Barkley is **very** big.

village A village is a small town.

When the Count was born, his parents announced the news to all the people who lived in the **village.**

1... One Baby Count!

violin A violin is a musical instrument. It has four strings and is played with a bow. Look up the word bow.

The Count loves to play the **violin.**

visit When you visit, you go to see someone or something.

Prairie Dawn likes to **visit** the museum.

DON'T TOUCH!

voice Your voice is the sound you make while talking or shouting or singing.

Hello, Bird!

I can hear Mr. Snuffle-upagus' **voice.**

Vacation is a word that begins with V. I would be very glad to take a vacation from this dictionary.

Ww

A B C D E F G H I J K L M N O P Q R S T U V **W** X Y Z

wagon   A wagon is used to carry things. A wagon has four wheels and is usually pulled.

wait   When you wait, you stop what you are doing or stay where you are until something happens.

Fred has to **wait** for Farmer Grover to load the **wagon.**

YAWN!

waiter   A waiter is a person who takes orders and serves food in a restaurant.

Waiter! What is this fly doing in my soup?

He is doing the backstroke, sir.

Grover the **waiter** is serving alphabet soup.

wake   When you wake, you stop sleeping.

Wake up, Ernie! The Late Pigeon News is over. It's time to go to bed.

walk When you walk, you move by taking steps.

Grover Knover's motorcycle is broken. He has to **walk.**

wall A wall is the side of a building or a room. A wall can also be a kind of fence.

Biff and Sully are painting the **walls** of the room blue.

Oscar is building a **wall** around his trash can.

I **want** a **wall** around my trash can so people won't bother me.

want When you want something, you would like to have it.

warm When something is warm, it is more hot than cold. But it is not *very* hot.

The water in the bathtub is **warm—** just right for Rubber Duckie and me.

was Ernie **was** dirty. Now he is clean.

wash When you wash something, you clean it with water and sometimes soap.

Betty Lou likes to **wash** Barkley. Barkley does not like to be **washed.**

waste   When you waste something, you do not make good use of it.

watch   A watch is a small clock that you can wear on your wrist or carry in your pocket. A watch shows you what time it is.

Bert has a **watch** on his wrist.

watch   When you watch something, you look at it.

Bert likes to **watch** the sun rise.

water   Water is wet. We use water to drink, to cook with, and to clean with. All living things need water.

Herry Monster is taking a bath in hot **water**. He is drinking a glass of cold **water**.

way   The way you do something is how you do it.

This is the **way** Ernie makes his bed.

This is the **way** Bert makes his bed.

way   The way you go is the direction or path in which you move.

we   We is another way of saying you and I.

weak   Something that is weak breaks easily or is not strong.

The toy wagon is **weak**. It will not hold Barkley.

wear   When you wear something, you have it on your body.

Marshal Grover **wears** a hat, a vest, chaps, and a shiny badge.

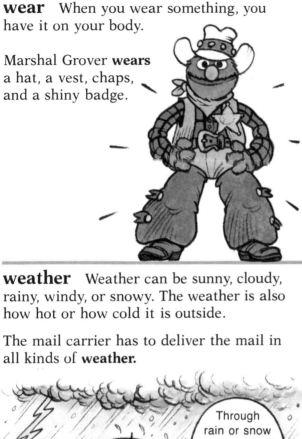

weather   Weather can be sunny, cloudy, rainy, windy, or snowy. The weather is also how hot or how cold it is outside.

The mail carrier has to deliver the mail in all kinds of **weather.**

> Through rain or snow or sleet or hail, I see that Sesame Gulch gets the mail.

week   A week is seven days long. Each day in the week has a special name. Look up the word calendar.

Bert has a busy **week.**

SUNDAY — Take Bernice for a walk.
MONDAY — Work on my bottle cap collection.
TUESDAY — Work on my paper clip collection.
WEDNESDAY — Buy oatmeal.
THURSDAY — Clean closet.
FRIDAY — Go to Pigeon Lovers' meeting.
SATURDAY — Polish saddle shoes.

weigh   When you weigh something, you find out how heavy it is.

weight   The weight of something is how heavy it is. Your weight is how heavy you are.

> Stand still, Farley. I want to **weigh** you. This scale will tell me your **weight.**

well   When you are well, you are not sick. You are healthy.

Farley is **well.**

> You are very healthy, Farley.

> When you do something **well,** you do it in a good way.

> I roller skate **well.**

were   The Busby twins **were** at the zoo.

> We **were** both at the zoo yesterday.

> You **were** there, too.

wet When something is wet, it has water or another liquid on it. It is not dry.

Barkley is **wet.**

Now everyone is **wet.**

whale A whale is a huge animal that lives in the ocean and looks like a fish. But it is not a fish. A whale breathes air.

The dictionary says that a **whale** looks like a fish but is not a fish.

AQUARIUM

what What is a word used to ask questions or talk about people and things.

What are you holding behind your back?

I have **what** my mother gave me for lunch.

wheel A wheel is something that is shaped like a circle and can roll or turn.

Three of these things belong together. One of these things is not the same.

The wagon, the tricycle, and the roller skates are all things that have **wheels.** The sled does not have **wheels.** The sled does not belong.

when When is a word used to ask questions or talk about time.

When does Cookie Monster *not* want a cookie?

When he wants *two* cookies!

where Where is a word used to ask questions or talk about places.

Where do you go to buy clothes?

I go **where** all the monsters go— to the Monster Department Store.

THE MONSTER DEPT. STORE

which Which is a word used to ask questions or talk about people or things.

Which pair of shoes do you want?

I know **which** pair— the pair that fits me.

while While means during the time of.

whisper When you whisper, you say something very quietly.

Ernie has to **whisper** **while** the Pigeon News is on.

Ernie! Don't make any noise **while** I am watching the Pigeon News.

Rubber Duckie, you're the one . . .

whistle A whistle is something that makes a loud, shrill sound when air is blown through it.

Herry Monster likes to blow his **whistle.**

whistle When you whistle, you make a loud, shrill sound by blowing air through your lips in a special way.

Sully likes to **whistle** while he works.

who Who is a word used to ask questions or talk about people.

Who lost this feather? The bird **who** lost this feather must be very big.

whole The whole of something is all the parts of it together.

I have a **whole** orange.

I have half an orange.

whose   Whose is a word used to ask questions or talk about things that belong to people.

why   Why is a word used to ask or talk about the reason for something.

wide   How wide something is means how far it is from one side to the other. When something is wide, it is not narrow.

wife   A wife is a woman who is married.

will   If you will do something, you are going to do it.

win When you win a game or a race, you finish ahead of the others.

wind Wind is air that is moving.

window A window is an opening in a building or a vehicle to let in air or light. Most windows have glass in them.

Bert is looking out the **window.**

wing A wing is the part of birds, bats, and some insects that helps them fly. Airplanes also have wings.

winter Winter is the name of a season. Winter comes after fall.

> I see snow on the ground. It must be **winter.**

Snuffle-upagus

with With means using or having. With also means in the company of.

> I keep the rain off **with** my rain hat.

> I have an umbrella **with** red stripes.

> Can I get under your umbrella **with** you?

wish A wish is something that you hope will come true. When you wish for something, you want it.

> Make a **wish** and blow out the candles.

> I **wish** everyone could be here to help me celebrate my birthday.

woman A woman is a grown-up girl.
There is one **woman,** one girl, and one monster in the elevator.

witch A witch is a person with magical powers. Many fairy tales have witches in them.

Connie the **witch** is reading a story.

> Once upon a time there was a clever, good, beautiful **witch** named Connie.

WITCH STORY

wonder When you wonder about something, you would like to know about it.

> There is just one thing I **wonder** about, Fred. What has happened to your head?

> I **wonder** if Marshal Grover will ever learn how to ride a horse.

wonderful Something wonderful is surprising or amazing. Sometimes the word wonderful is used to mean very good.

That's **wonderful!**

wood Wood is the hard part of a tree. Many things are made of wood.

I like to build things with **wood.**

word A word is a group of letters or sounds that has a meaning. You can say a word or read it.

There are so many **words** that begin with W. WOW!

work When you work, you do something that uses energy. Most people work at jobs to earn money.

Special

I **work** at the post office.

U.S. MAIL

I **work** at the grocery store.

I **work** at the hospital.

I **work** at the factory.

I **work** at school.

MATH

I am not **working.** I am resting.

world A world is a planet. Our world is the planet earth.

I can see the whole **world** from my little spaceship.

worm A worm is a tiny animal with a long, soft body and no legs. Earthworms live under the ground.

Slimey is my pet **worm.**

worry When you worry, you are afraid that something bad is going to happen.

Be careful, Ernie! Those cups are going to fall.

You **worry** too much, Bert.

wrap When you wrap something, you cover it.

I have to **wrap** this present for Mr. Snuffle-upagus.

write When you write, you put words on something—usually paper.

writer A writer is someone who writes stories, letters, or other things for people to read.

Herry is a **writer.** Does he **write** with his left hand or his right hand?

I **write** with a pencil.

wrong When something is wrong, it is not correct. It is not true.

Farley has four apples. Right or **wrong**?

Wrong! I have only three apples.

I wonder where the words wart, weed, whimper, and whine went.

X x Y y Z z

x-ray   An x-ray is a picture of the inside of something. Sometimes the doctor takes an x-ray of your body to see if anything is wrong inside.

The doctor took an **x-ray** of Mr. Hooper's chest.

xylophone   A xylophone is a musical instrument with two rows of wooden bars that you hit with wooden hammers.

Frazzle likes to play the **xylophone.**

yard   A yard is a piece of ground next to a house or a school or another kind of building.

Biff and Sully are building a fence around their **yard.**

yawn   When you yawn, you open your mouth wide and take a deep breath. You yawn because you are tired or bored.

And I found this bottle cap on the sidewalk one day when I was walking home from the store. I had just bought some oatmeal . . . .

Bert's stories make Ernie **yawn.**

year A year is an amount of time that is three hundred and sixty-five days long. A new year begins with January and ends with December. Look up the word calendar.

Today is my birthday. Now I will have to wait a whole **year** for my next birthday.

yell When you yell, you cry out loudly.

Cookie Monster **yells** KOWABUNGA when he sees a pile of cookies.

KOWABUNGA!

yes Yes is a word you use to say that something is true. You can also use yes to say you will or can do something.

Cookie Monster, do you want a cookie?

YES!

yesterday Yesterday is the day that came before today.

Yesterday I washed the clothes.

Today I am ironing them.

you You means the person or persons spoken to.

This belongs to **you**, Ernie.

These belong to **you**, Bert.

young Someone who is young has lived a short time. A young person has not lived as long as someone who is old.

Farley is **young**, but his baby brother is **younger**. Their grandfather is old.

Baby Brother

Farley

Grandfather

your Your is another way of saying belonging to you.

yours When something belongs to you, it is yours.

Is this **your** umbrella, Little Bird?

Yes, that's mine. Is this **yours**?

yourself Yourself is sometimes used instead of you.

Mommy, I fell down.

Did you hurt **yourself**, Grover, dear?

Yo-Yo™ A Yo-Yo is a toy that goes up and down on a string.

Betty Lou is trying to win the **Yo-Yo** contest.

zebra A zebra is a white animal with black stripes. A zebra has four legs, a mane, and a tail.

Zebras look like striped horses.

And most of us live in Africa.

zipper A zipper is something that is used to fasten clothes or other things.

Ernie, please help me **zip** the **zipper** on my jacket.

Sure, Bert. But first I have to un**zip** the **zipper** on my sleeping bag.

ZIP!

ZOO A zoo is a place where animals are kept so that people can see them.

Big Bird likes to visit the animals at the **zoo.**